THIS BOOK IS DEDICATED TO
MY MOTHER,
PAULA MAYO, AND
MY SISTER,
SHAVON MAYO.

I LOVE YOU BOTH SO MUCH.

The summer of 2010 I was living around Trinidad, on Meigs Place NE. I was 13 years old when I moved there. I was nervous about moving to Trinidad because my hood, 21st and Vietnam, was beefing with Trinidad. I knew if they asked me where I'm from and I say "21st and Vietnam" they were going to jump me. I did not want to move to Trinidad because we were leaving my hood, where I was from, where I knew everybody. I grew up on 21st until I was 12 years old.

The neighborhood has apartment complexes with four apartment buildings, two in the back and two in the front. Each building has about nine apartments. The bricks on the building are burgundy. If you don't live in the complex, you have to buzz to get in. Every day kids come outside and play, all through the seasons. Moms come outside and conversate.

When I first moved around Trinidad, I was walking to the store with Tay. He is my neighbor Piggy's nephew.

A group of boys came up to us and said, "Where ya'll from?"

I said, "21st Street"

When I looked into the group of boys, I remembered one of the boy's faces because I used to go to Brown High School with him.

One of the boys said, "He just said he's from 21st."

I said, "Yeah, that's where I'm from, OTF."

Then he said, "You got to see me." I put my mother's bags down with the cereal and milk in it. Then we started to square up.

The boy I used to go to school with said, "Leave him alone. I used to go to school with him, he good."

All of a sudden, Tay ran. The boys said they didn't want to fight me. They wanted Tay because they could have jumped me and he ran. They ran after him. I picked my bags up and went through the alley on

Simms Place and walked on to Raum Street. Then I was on Meigs Place, in front of my house. I walked up the stairs and went in the house and called out,

"Mom, Guess what just happened?"

She said, "What?"

"I was walking to the store and this group of boys came up to me. Tay ran on me. I could have got jumped but they ran after him."

She said, "That's messed up."

I started to laugh. I walked in my room, pulled out a backwood and two Js of loud and rolled up. When I was done, I pulled out my lighter and lit the J and faced it.

When I was done smoking, I was high as could be, so I walked out of my room and called out,

"Ma!"

She didn't answer.

I said, "Ma" again and she still didn't answer. I knew where she was. She was downstairs, over Piggy's house. I went down there, opened the door, went in, and closed the door behind me. Then I walked in the back to Piggy's room and Piggy, my mother and Ooni, Piggy's sister, were sitting on the bed. They weretalking about how her nephew, Tay, ran on me when I was about to fight.

My mom is about 5'7", brown-skinned, with pretty brown eyes. My mom and I have a pretty good relationship because she raised me my whole life, and I respect her. I like to watch movies and go out to the mall with my mother. My mother does not have strict rules. The only things I have to do are: take out the trash, wash the dishes, and clean my room. I don't break her rules.

Piggy is my mother's best friend. She likes to have fun. She likes to get high and listen to music. She is a thick person. She is brown-skinned. She dresses ok. She likes her pants to hug her, so she can look *phat*. She has a sexy voice.

I said, "Ma, I'll be back later. I'm about to go around the way and chill."

She said, "Aight. If you don't come in tonight, call and let me know."

"Okay Mom. I love you."

"I love you, too."

I left out of Piggy's house, walked down the stairs, turned right, walked across Trinidad Avenue and kept going straight, passing through Trinidad Recreation Center. Then, I saw one of the boys that I was about to fight.

He said, "Wassup?"

I said, "Nothin', coolin"

He said, "I thought you was going to run, but you stood your ground even though you from 21 and our hoods are beefing. But, your man- he's wild."

I said, "I'm hip."

He said, "My name is Derico."

"My name is Lil-B"

"Aight, I'm going to see you around sometime, Lil-B."

I said, "Aight then."

I turned around, walked down towards Bladensburg Rd., across to L Street, and down 19th Street. As I was walking down 19th Street, I saw my man Justin.

He said, "Fire up or match a J of loud?"

I said, "Match one."

He walked up Langston with me so I could get a J from one of our men. Then, we walked to a corner store called Food 7, and got two backwoods. We walked to Justin's house, right up the alley from Food 7, and went in the basement and rolled up. Then we sparked one J up. After that J was gone, John Boy walked in. That's Justin's twin brother.

John Boy said, "Match me one."

Justin said, "Aight bet."

While John Boy was rolling, Justin sparked his jay and said "Three-P?"

We both said, "Aight."

We were smoking. We were all high as can be in the basement.

I started smoking weed when I was five. I started with my grandmother. I do it because it makes me feel good, and it makes my stress go away. A lot of my friends, aunts, and uncles smoke weed too. The good thing about weed is it makes you feel good and your stress goes away for that moment. The bad thing about weed is your brain cells die and sometimes you get master headaches. It is illegal to sell weed. I got locked up once for distribution (trying to sell it). I got charged with distribution on 9/29/2010.

Weed is a small offense. The people that I know are not afraid or nervous to use it. Some drug dealers don't like to have a lot on them. But when I used to sell weed, I kept all my weed on me. Smoking marijuana is legal now in DC, but I think nothing's going to change.

After all the Js were gone, we walked outside. Justin said he was going to hit a move. I didn't want to go. I already had like $500, so I was good for a minute. John-Boy and I walked up the street on H Place to Tray-Tray's house.

I walked to the window and said, "Ma Sugar- where Tray-Tray at?"

She said, "In his room. The front door is open."
John-Boy and I walked in and went to Tray-Tray's room. He was playing the X-Box 360.

Tray- Tray said, "Was' up Lil B and Twin?"

We both said, "Was' up?"
We sat down on his bed.

Tray-Tray said, "Lil-B, go in the living room and look under the table and get the wooden box."

I said, "Aight."
I went and got the box, came back and gave it to him.

He said, "Look in my coat pocket and get them 3 grape cigarillos."
I went in his pocket, grabbed them, and gave them to him.

I said, "Let me play."

He said, "Aight."

He gave me the controller and I started to play the game. Then I looked in the wooden box. There was a lot of weed.

I said, "Damm."
I turned around and started playing the game again.

I started playing video games when I was about six. The first game I ever played was 007 on Nintendo 64. I like shooting games or racing games and Grand Theft Auto. Playing video games makes me feel good. I like to play video games because they're fun, and they keep me out of trouble.

While I was playing the game, Tray-Tray was rolling up. Then he sparked the J, hit it a couple of times, and passed it to me. I did the same thing and passed it to John Boy. I started to get chased on the game by the cops, and then I died. So I passed the controller to Twin. Then we heard a knock on Tray-Tray's window. He pulled his blinds up. In front of his window, it was John-Boy's twin brother, Justin, BK, and Charlie.

Tray said, "Hold up." We were about to come outside because there would be too many people in his house. We went out back where everybody was at. It was *live* that day out back at Tray-Tray's house. It was me, Tray-Tray, both of the twins, BK, Charlie, V-man, Vaneda, Trayvell, Loss, and some other people. It was *too live* to remember everybody's name. We were *turnt.* (**Turnt** means to drink, smoke, relax, laugh with your friends, and play music.)

The weather was sunny, hot, and humid. My friends and I got together like this a lot- to smoke and drink. All my friends have good personalities, but sometimes they got their days. We were drinking Lean and New Amsterdam vodka. People were wearing shorts, tank tops, and some were wearing pants and short-sleeve shirts. Some people were standing, and some were dancing. People were talking about all kinds of things. There was endless weed going around in rotation, endless bottles going around, music playing, girls dancing, and all that good **"turnt"** stuff.

When it was about 7:00 in the evening, I said, "It's time for me to go home."

I walked up 19th Street, made a left onto L Street and walked until I was on Bladensberg Road. Then, I made a right on Bladensberg and walked up Mount Olivet Road until I hit Trinidad Avenue. I made a left on Trinidad and walked to Meigs Place. I made a right on Meigs and my house was right there. I walked up my stairs, opened my door, went in the house, locked the door behind me, went to my mother's room, and lay on the bed with my mother and my little sister, Shay-Shay. Now, it was about 7:30.

My mother had cooked some fried chicken and some rice and corn. I smelled it in the hallway. It smelled so good. I ate. Then I went in my room, rolled me up a J, and smoked. After I was done smoking, I fell asleep.

Shay-Shay is a nickname. Her real name is Shavon. My little sister is six years old, ten years younger than me. She is brown-skinned with pretty long hair. My mother likes to cook fried chicken, macaroni and cheese, and rice. These are my favorite foods. Sometimes, I cook with her.

I woke up the next morning to some hot breakfast. After I ate, it was about 9:00 in the morning. I took a shower, brushed my teeth, put on some deodorant, and brushed my hair. I told my mother I was going outside.

She said, "OK."

I walked out the front door. I walked to my man Coda's house on West Virginia Avenue and knocked on his door. His mother came to the door.

"Who is it?" she called.

I answered, "It's Lil-B, Ma."

She opened the door and let me in.

I asked, "Where Coda at?"

"In his room."

I walked to the back, opened his door, and said, "Coda, getcha ass up."

He got up.

I asked him, "Do you have a roll up?"

"No, but I got a J already rolled."

He got his J from under his desk and sparked it up.

I said, "Coda, we need a move."

He said, "I'm sharp."

Then his mother came back in his room.

"Can I hit that jay?" she asked.

I passed it to her. "Ma, you got a roll-up?"

She said yes, went to her room, and got a chocolate cigarillo. She came back to Coda's room and threw me the roll-up. Then, she passed the J to Coda. I broke down the roll-up and started to roll. By the time I was done rolling the new J, the other one was halfway gone. Coda put it out, gave it to his mother, and told her she could have it.

She said, "Okay" and walked to her room.

Coda started to put his clothes on. When he was done, we walked out the back door that he had in his room. We started to walk down the alley that led us to Mount Olivet Road. We made a right on Mount Olivet Road and walked towards the Circle 7. Once we got by the store, we posted up and sparked the J that I was rolling in the house. Coda and I were ping-ponging the J back and forth. Then, our friends Darren and Smiley walked up. They gave us some dap.

Darren said, "We got four or five Js, but we need a roll up."

I said, "Aight" and walked behind the store to Simms Place.

My uncle was up the street, so I walked up there and asked him, "What's up?"

He said, "Nothin'- coolin'. Tryin' to make this money."

I said, "I'm hip. But can I have five dollars right quick?"

"I got you," he said and pulled out one stack with all hundred dollar bills.

He said, "Wrong stack" and put it back in his pocket. He pulled out another stack with fifties, twenties, tens, and fives. He didn't have any ones. He gave me ten dollars.

I said, "Thank you."

He said, "You good, nephew" so I stepped off. I got halfway down the street and heard somebody say, "Hey, Lil B."

I turned around. It was my uncle.

He said, "Come back."

I walked back up there and he said,

"Shawty, you can't keep asking people for money. You got to find a hustle somewhere, somehow. That 10 dollars I just gave you is play money, but take this two hundred dollars and find a hustle."

I said, "Aight, bet, good looking."

"No problem, nephew."

I walked back down the street, went back to the Circle 7 and gave Darren the ten dollar bill so he could get three roll-ups. He went into the store, got them, came back out, and gave me my change back. All of us walked behind the store on Simms, where Smiley lived. We walked in his house and went straight to the back, to his room. Darren started to roll up a J. When he was done, he sparked the J and hit it three times. Then he passed it to me. I hit the J four times and passed it to Coda. He did the same thing and passed it to

Smiley. The J went around a couple of times. Then it was gone.

I told Darren to give me a roll up so I could roll. I pearled the J. When I was done, I sparked the J up. Then Darren asked me if I wanted to play him in 2K-13. That's a basketball video game, if you don't know.

I said, "Yeah."

Then I passed him the J, while he gave me the controller to the X-Box 360 and turned the game on. We started by picking our teams. I had 94-97 Bulls with Michael Jordan. He picked OKC and we started to play. I don't remember who won that game. But after the game, Coda and I walked outside. It was about 4:00 in the afternoon. I asked Coda if he knew somebody we could get an ounce of weed from.

He said, "Yeah."

We walked to his man's house on Raum Street and knocked on his door. He opened it, and we walked in.

He said, "What's up, Coda?"

Coda said, "Shit- coolin. But I need an ounce."

He said, "Aight. Bet." I gave Coda one hundred dollars, and he gave it to his man. His man went in the back room. When he came back, he threw the ounce to Coda.

Then, we walked out. We walked to Coda's house on West Virginia Ave because he said he had some weed bags. We bagged up $225 worth of weed. That's how much you bag up with an ounce.

After we were done, we walked back outside, around Simms Place. We posted up on Smiley's front porch. That's where all the weed-heads come and get their weed from.

About thirty minutes went past and six sales came for $20 worth of weed each.

I made the sales and gave all my weed to my right hand man, Coda. I told him to sell the weed and give me the money.

He said, "Aight."

His phone rang, and he answered it. He told me it was his man calling to say that he wanted $50 worth of weed.

I said, "Aight, bet. Where he at?"

"On his way over here. He's on West Virginia Avenue."

We waited for like 10 or 15 minutes and he walked up and said, "Wassup Coda?"

Coda said, "Coolin'. Trying to make this money."

"Kill. But let me get that."

Coda made the sale.

His man said, "Be careful because them boys out here heavy."

Coda said, "I'm hip, but good looking out."

His man walked off and we stayed on the porch on Simms Place. I told Coda to go and get a roll up so I could spark a J.

He said, "Aight."

Coda walked to the Circle 7, got a roll up, and came back to the porch. I asked Coda to break down the roll up because he was going to roll the J.

He said, "Okay."

I pulled the weed out of my pocket and broke it down. Then, I gave him the weed and he started to roll the J up. Coda always likes to roll the J, so I let him do it most of the time. When we were done smoking, I told him I was going to see him in the morning because I needed to re-up.

He said, "Aight, bet."

I told him to give me the rest of the weed that was left and started to walk up Simms Place. I made a right into the alley, left on Raum Street, then made a right into another alley. I walked to the end of that alley and my house was on the corner. I walked up my steps and knocked on my door.

My little sister asked, "Who is it?"

I responded, "It's me, Shay-Shay." She said, "Oh" and opened the door. I walked in, closed the door behind me, and locked it.

I asked Shay, "Where's Ma at?"

She said, "In the room, asleep."

I said, "Ok."

I went in the freezer and got a pizza and cooked it in the oven. I made some purple Kool-aid after my pizza was done. I ate and drank some Kool-aid and took a shower. I put on my army fatigue long johns. Then, I asked my sister if she was hungry.

She said, "Yeah."

"What do you want me to make you?"

"I want some cereal."

I said, "Ok" and fixed her a bowl of Capn' Crunch. She ate and went in my mother's room and went to bed. I checked all the windows and doors to make sure they were locked, like I do every night. Then I walked in my room and went to sleep.

The next morning I woke up around 11:00, went in the bathroom to brush my teeth and wash my face.

My mother asked me, "Do you want some breakfast?"

I said, "No, I'm good."
I went in my room, put on my all white Air Force Ones with my black and white Adidas sweatpants and my black and white Adidas shirt. I like Adidas, Gucci, H & M, Polo, Tommy Hilfiger, Nautica, and Versace. Clothes are important in my community because if you are not fly, the girls will call you dirty. When I get a new outfit, I feel like the man.

I walked to my mother's room and told her and Shay,

"I'll see ya'll later." I gave my mother and my little sister a kiss and walked out of the house. As I walked out of the house, I saw Derico walking towards the Rec.

I called him, "Hey, Derico."

He turned around, "What's up Lil B? What you about to do?"

"Nothing."

He said, "Walk with me to the Rec."

"Aight bet, c'mon."

We started walking towards the Rec Center. When we got to the Rec, we went inside, walked to the gym and started to play 3-on-3 basketball. It was me, Derico, and Debo on a team against DeAngelo (Derico's brother) and two other guys. As we were playing, a group of girls came in the gym. Only one girl got my attention, so I kept playing basketball.

After the game was over, Derico, his brother, and I all walked outside where the girls were. They were asking, "What's my name?" because they knew everyone else, but they didn't know me.

I said, "Lil B".

Then I realized that I was supposed to go to Coda's house this morning.

I asked, "What time it is?"

Somebody said, "3:00"

I told Derico I'd see him later.

He said, "Aight."

I walked back towards my house, made a right on Trinidad Avenue, walked two blocks to Simms Place, and made a left. I walked down the street and Coda and Smiley were on the porch smoking a J and a cigarette.

I walked up and asked, "Can I hit that cigarette?"

Coda passed me the jack.

I said, "C'mon Coda, we need to go and hit that move."

He said, "Aight. C'mon."

It took us like 5 or 10 minutes to go to his

man's house. When we got there, Coda knocked on his door.

"Who is it?" somebody called from inside.

"It's Coda."

His man opened the door and said, "What's up?"

Coda said, "Trying to make this money."

"I know that's right."
Coda said, "Give me another ounce."

"Aight. Hold on."
He walked in the back.
I gave Coda a hundred dollars for the weed.

His man came back in the living room and said, "I put some extras in there too."

Coda said, "Good lookin'."
Then we rolled out. We walked back to Smiley's porch and rolled up a J. As we were smoking, the group of girls from the Rec walked past and one of them said, "Lil

B, the one right here in the middle likes you."

I said, "Oh true." They walked on to the store.

Coda said, "Go smack. She is cute and all that."

I said, "I'm hip."

They walked back past and I went up to the girl who they said liked me.

I asked her what her name was.

She said, "Aleah" with a smile on her face.

I said, "True."

Then she asked me what my name was.

"They call me Lil' B."

"Oh."

"Can I call you sometime?"

She said, "Yeah" and gave me her number: 202-491-5565.

"Aight, I'm going to call you later on."

"Make sure you do that."

"Aight, Beautiful."

I walked back to the porch where Coda was.

I said, "Bruhh, I'm about to go back in the house."

"Aight, bag the weed up."

"Aight bruhh I'm gonna do that." I started to walk up the street and saw my uncle. I went to him and asked for a hundred block of some coke.

He said, "Go to my truck and get it out of the arm rest and throw the hundred dollars on the floor."

I said, "Aight."

I got in his all white Range Rover, counted my money, and threw the hundred dollars on the floor. I went in the arm rest, got my coke, and got out.

Then I yelled to him, "I'm goin' in the house."

He said, "Aight, be safe." I went in the house, took a shower, ate, and went to sleep. I woke up the next morning and started to clean my room.

When I was done, I went in my mother's room and grabbed a cigarette. Then I walked back in my room, locked my door, went in my closet, and grabbed my weed. I sat down on my bed and started to bag it up at my table. When I was done, I had bagged up $275 worth of weed. I put the weed in a big Ziploc bag. Then I started to get dressed.

After I got dressed, I grabbed my weed and my coke that I hadn't bagged up yet. Then, I lit my cigarette and walked outside. I went down the street to Coda's house and knocked on his back door.

He opened the door and I said, "What's up?"

"Nothing, Coolin. Did you bag that up?"

"Yeah, but I need to bag this coke up."

"You lying."

So I threw it on his bed.

He said, "You stepped your game up?"

I said, "Yeah. There's money in these streets and we need it. Do you got some coke bags?"

"No, but they are $5 at the gas station."

"Aight."

I gave him $5 and he went to the gas station to buy the coke bags. When he came back in the house, we both started to bag the coke up. We bagged up $210 worth of coke. After that I told him that he's going to sell the coke, while I sell the weed.

He said, "Aight."

We walked outside to the Northeast Market and posted up for a good ten minutes. Then I made three sales. After that, I saw this crackhead named Tony who told me everything I knew about Trinidad. Tony wasn't a dirty crackhead. Usually, crackheads' clothes are dirty. They make sounds you've never heard before. They keep playing with their nose and scratching their necks. They will do anything to get their next high. You may wonder how I felt about doing this? When I used to sell coke, I felt like, "Damm, I'm killing my own kind with this poison.

I said, "Tony, come here."

He walked over to me and said, "What's up B?"

I said, "I got some coke and stuff I need to get off, and I need your help."

He said, "Aight."

I told Coda to give him a dime of coke. Coda gave it to him and Tony said, "I'm going to tell you what your stuff is hitting on."

I said, "Aight."

Half an hour went past. It was around 6:30. My man Coda and I still had a lot of weed and coke left. I looked at Coda and said, "It's getting late."

"I'm hip."

Then he lit a jack up so I said, "Let me deuce that."

He said, "Aight bet."

We saw Tony walking our way.

He called out, "Lil B, come here."

Coda and I walked over there to see what he wanted.

He said, "That stuff is some good-good."

I said, "Kill. That's all I needed to know."

He said, "I'm going to send ya'll some sales."

Coda and I both said, "Aight".

We walked back to the store. Then, out of nowhere, five fiends came to Coda and said, "Let me get two."

He said, "Aight, walk to the alley on Simms Place."

One fiend turned around and walked towards the alley. The other fiends followed. Then Coda passed me the jack and followed after them. After he gave the crackheads their crack, he came back to the store where I was and said, "Them' fiends stink."

I started to laugh. I said, "Bruhh' I'm about to go in the house."

He said, "Me too, once you leave." I gave Coda some dap and told him I'm gonna see him tomorrow. I told him he could keep the coke in case he came out first.

He said, "Aight, little bruhh'." Then we both walked our separate ways. From where I was, it took me about five minutes to get to my house.

When I went in the house, my mother had her friends, Don, Von, and Ron, in the living room. I know those names sound unusual, but those are their real names. Don and Von are a couple. My mother has known them for years.

I walked in and said, "What's up?"

They said, "What's up?"

I went in my room and changed into my army fatigue pajamas. I've had them since I was little and I could still fit them.

Then I went back to the living room and asked my mother if I could see her phone.

She said, "Yeah, it's on the charger in my room, at the end of my bed."

I went to her room and got her phone. It was an Iphone 4S. I walked to my room, closed my door, and turned my TV on to BET. Martin was on, so I lay on my bed and called Aleah.

This is what I knew about Aleah: She is brown-skinned, stands at 5' 5" with a shape like a model. She has a nice-sized butt, and her hair comes to her shoulders. She changes her hair up a lot. She always dresses in style; her clothes always look good. She talks sexy. She doesn't smoke or drink. Her eyes are light brown. She has a beautiful smile. The day I met her was the first time I'd seen her. We do not have friends in common. We do not hang out with the same people. I liked her right away because she's funny, she's cute, and she has a good personality. She gets mad easily. For example, we can be on the phone talking and she'll say something in a low voice.

I'll say, "What'd you say?"
She'll say it again, but still low and I won't hear her.

I'll ask, "What'd you say again?"
She'll say, "Nuthin!" in a mad voice!
She has a best friend, and her name is Alexia.

I dialed her number: 202-491-5565. It rang like two or three times and somebody picked up and said hello.

I said, "Can I speak to Aleah?"
"This is her. Who is this?"
"This is Lil B."
"Oh, you just calling me?! I gave you my number like two days ago."
"My bad, Baby Girl, I've been busy."
"Oh, aight."

"So what, you have been waiting on my call or something?"

"Something like that."

"True. That's cute. I'm trying to be more than friends."

"Oh, you is? Huh?"

"Yeah, so what's up?"

"Let me think about it for the rest of the night, and I'll tell you tomorrow. Just meet me at the Rec around 10 or 11."

"Aight, bet. But I've been doing a lot of running around today, and I'm tired. So I'm going to call you when I wake up in the morning to meet you at the Rec."

Aleah said, "Aight."

I said, "Good night."

She said it back.

Then we both hung up the phone. After we got off the phone, I yelled from behind my closed door, "Shay!"

She said, "What?"

I said, "Come and get Ma's phone."

She said, "Aight."

She came in my room and got the phone from me and said, "Good night, bro, I love you."

I said, "Good night, Sis, I love you more."

She walked out and closed my door. When I looked at the TV, Martin was still on. I started to watch TV. As I was watching, I fell asleep. The next morning I woke up around 9am. I got out of my bed, grabbed my toothbrush and my washcloth for my face, went to the bathroom, brushed my teeth and washed my face. After I was done, I went back into my room and went to my closet. I grabbed a tee-shirt, my underwear, and my AXE Phoenix body wash, and went to the bathroom to take a shower. I was in the shower for about 30-45 minutes. When I got out, I dried off and put my underwear and tee-shirt on. I went into my room, went back to my closet to pick out my clothes that I was going to wear today. I grabbed my blue and green polo shirt and my green army fatigue H & M pants, with my blue and green Jordans. After I picked out my clothes, I went to my mother's room and got her phone. I walked back to my room. By now, it was around 10:00 in the morning. As I was putting my clothes on, I dialed Aleah's number.

She answered on the second ring and said, "Hello."

I said, "What's up, Aleah?"

"Coolin. I'm like five minutes away from the Rec."

"A'ight bet. I'm going to meet you there in ten minutes."

"Aight."

We both hung up the phone. I went back into my mother's room to give her the phone back. I told her that I was about to go outside.

She said, "Aight."

Then, I told her I love her.

She said, "I love you, too."

When Aleah said Yes that she would be my girl, I felt like the most important person in the world.

I went back into my room to get the rest of my weed. Then, I left out of the house. I walked downstairs and knocked on Piggy's door. I asked her for a cigarette.

She said, "Hold up" and walked back into her house, came back, and gave me a cigarette.

I said, "Thanks" and turned around and walked towards the Rec. When I got to the Rec, Aleah was outside with her sister, Dashawn. When I got close to them, I said, "What's up?" to both of them and gave Aleah a hug. Then Dashawn went into the Rec while Aleah and I started to talk.

Aleah asked, "Why do you want me to be your girlfriend?"

I said, "Because you're pretty, and you seem like a good girl, and you aren't the type to get in trouble."

She smiled, "True. But, to tell you the truth, I like you too and I want to be your girlfriend."

I said, "For real?" with a smile on my face.

She said, "Yeah, I'm for real."

Then, after we stopped talking, I said, "Boo, I'm sorry but I've got to do something for my mother."

She said, "It's okay" and she gave me a hug.

Then I said, "If I'm done early, then I'll call you to see if you're still up here, so I can come and chill with you."

She said, "Aight."

I turned around and walked back towards my house on Meigs Place. I made a right in the alley on Meigs, walked down to Raum Street, made a left on Raum, walked down

Raum, made a right into another alley, walked down to Simms, then made a left, then made another right, walked through the alley behind Kovack's Liquor Store and walked by the Circle 7. Coda was sitting on the wall in front of the store.

I went to him and said, "What's up?"

"Nothing, trying to get this money."

"Oh yeah, that's a bet."

"Wassup with you though?"

"Nothing, just came from seeing Aleah at the Rec."

"True."

Then a crackhead came over where we were and she asked, "Coda, you still got that good stuff?"

"Yeah."

"Can I get 2 for 8?"

"Yeah, I got you, but next time I need straight money."

She said, "Aight"

Coda told her to go behind the store. She began to walk behind the store. Coda followed her and made the sale. He came back where I was.

I asked him, "How much money did you make so far?"

"$160"

I said, "Bet, let me get that."

He gave me the money. I already had $200 that I had made from selling the weed. Altogether we had $360, not even counting the rest of the weed and coke we still got.

I gave Coda $1.25 to get a chocolate cigarillo.

He said, "Aight," walked in the store, purchased the roll up, came back out and asked, "Where are we going to smoke at?"

"At the dungeon."

"Aight."

We walked to the dungeon that's behind Smiley's house. I told Coda to start rolling while I break down the weed. Then we started to smoke. It seemed like the jay was in rotation forever. After we were done smoking, we walked back on Simms Place and saw my little cousin, Loss. He said he had just moved around here, on Simms Place.

I asked, "Where at?"

Loss answered, "Right there by the alley."

I said, "Aight, bet. Where you about to go?"

He said, "With y'all."

Then Coda called from down the block,

"Lil B, c'mon. I think I got a sale."

Loss and I walked to the Northeast Market where Coda was.

He walked up to a crackhead and said, "I got that."

The crackhead said, "If Tay not around the corner, I'm going to come back and holler at you."

Coda said, "Alright, make sure you do that."

Then, a pretty lady came up to Coda and asked, "Do you know where the weed at?"

He said, "Yeah, my little man got it" and pointed towards me.

She came over to me, "Can I get two nicks?"

I said, "Yeah, I got that."
I told her to stay right there and I'll be right back. I walked behind the store, digged in my pants, and grabbed out two nicks that I had in a Ziploc bag. I waved at her to come and get it.

She said, "I have 9."

I said, "Aight."
Then she gave me the money and walked off. I stood right there and counted my money. It was $9.00.
I walked back where Coda and my little cousin, Loss, were.
They both were laughing.

I said, "What ya'll laughing at?"

Coda said, "Look over there, they fighting in the street."

I started to laugh too because there were two females falling and ripping each other's clothes off. It was unbelievable because they were older, and they tore off each other's shirts and bras. They were in the street bare-chested. Then they stopped and walked off without shirts and bras!

The crackhead that Coda went to earlier came back and said, "I got $25 for 3 joints."

Coda said, "Aight bet, hold on."

He walked behind the store, got the three joints, came back, and gave it to the crackhead. Then the crackhead gave Coda the money. Coda put the money in his pocket and walked where I was.

I said, "Bruhh, did you count the money?"

He said, "No, not yet, but I'm about to count it now."

Now it's like 6:30 at night. It started to get live at the Circle 7: endless females and endless wild N****

I saw this guy Coda and I knew, Fat D. He stopped and talked to us for a minute.

Then, he stepped off and said, "Ya'll, I'll be right back."

Coda said, "Aight."

Fat D walked back and asked, "Lil B, you still got some weed?"

"Yeah, I got 3 left."

"I got a sale for you."

"Oh yeah, where they at?"

"Right here."

Then he waved at two females to come over where we were standing.

As they were walking towards us, I said,

"D, they look like undercovers, bruhh?"

He said, "Nahh, they good."

Coda said, "They do look like undercovers, though."

D said, "If they are, and the police pull up, I'm going to throw you the money, Coda, so ya'll walk off."

Coda said, "Aight."

I gave D the two bags of tree. The two white females who D brought over to me saw me give D the weed. He made the sale. As soon as they walked off, five police cars pulled up, with their lights flashing, sirens blaring. The police pulled over and hopped out. D threw the money to Coda and we both stepped off. As the police were pressing D out, Coda and I got to the bottom of Raum Street.

Then the jump-outs saw me. They "jumped out" on me because the undercovers had given them my description.

I ran a little bit and tried to throw the last bag of weed I had over the fence. But they saw me and grabbed me. They put me on

the ground and put handcuffs on me.
Then, one of the police jumped over the
fence and got the bag of weed.

The police officer started to ask me
questions like:

"How old are you?"

" Where do you live?"

"Why you selling drugs at a young
age?"

"What's your mom's name and
number?"

After I gave it to them, they called her and
told her that I was getting locked up for
selling weed and that she needed to come
and get my property from the bottom of
Raum Street and Montello.

She said, "Okay."

There were a lot of people watching me
get locked up. It took my mother five
minutes to come where I was. When I saw
her, I started to cry because I was
ashamed.

When she got closer, she said, "Don't cry now because you seen me. You the one out here selling drugs." She started to talk to the police officer. They gave her my property. She looked at me and said, "I love you."

I said, "I love you too." But I was still crying a little bit. The police picked me up and put me in their squad car. They took me to YSC (Youth Services Center). That's a jail for juveniles who commit crimes in Washington DC. It's right in my own neighborhood, not even 10 minutes away.

When we got to the back of YSC, the police had to push a button for Control to open up the sally port. When we went into the sally port, we had to wait about three minutes for it to close. Then, a policeman came out who worked on the MPD (Metropolitan Police Department) side of YSC.

Once we got into YSC, I had to go over to the MPD side first to get mug shots and fingerprints. It took us an hour and a half to get all that done. After we were done, a female officer took me over to the YSC side so that I could do my intake over there. When I got over there, the YDR (Youth Development Representative) came to me and told me to take my shoes off. I took them off and gave them to the YDR. He turned them upside down and smacked them together. Then, he gave them back to me, and I put my shoes back on. He checked my pants pockets, and the search was done.

He asked me, "Are you hungry?"

I said, "Yeah."

Then he walked in the back and got two bologna sandwiches, Oreo cookies, and a juice.

I said, "Thank you."

He said, "You're welcome, go to Cell E."

I said, "Aight."

I was in Cell E for about two hours. I fell asleep and all of a sudden I heard a knock on the cell. One of the officers opened it and said, "Go to that room right there with the lady in it."

I walked over and she pointed to the chair that was on the other side of her desk and said, "Sit please."

When I sat down, she asked me what's my name.

I said, "Bryant Mayo."

Then she asked me what's my date of birth.

I said, "4/14/1997."

Then she read me the charge I was getting. It was Distribution of Marijuana. She asked me for my mother's number.

I said: 202-710-2667.

Then she called the number. The phone rang like 3 to 5 times before my mother answered. She said, "Hello?"

Then the lady said, "Is this Paula Mayo? Bryant Mayo's mother?"

She said, "Yes."

"I was calling you because your son is up at YSC. He was arrested about 4 hours ago."

"I know," she answered.

"I was calling to let you know that he got a court date next week on Wednesday."

My mom said, "Okay"

The lady continued, "Being as this is his first charge he is able to come home this morning. We are just waiting on transportation to come get him, and he will be dropped off at home."

My mother replied, "Thank you."

They both hung up the phone. Then the lady gave me a paper with my court date and case number on it. She said I was done and yelled out, "Bryant Mayo done at 4:00 a.m."

The staff told me to go back in my cell. I was in there for about 25 more minutes. Then I saw a van come through the sally port and stop. People got out and came into YSC.

One man said, "We are here to take Bryant Mayo home."

The YSC staff called me and said, "Come out."

I came out of my cell.

The staff said, "Put your back on the wall." I did what they asked. It took us two more minutes to get the paper work so I could leave. When we got the paper work, we left out of the sally port and when I got in the van it was 4:30 in the morning. I was tired. The transportation crew asked me where I lived.

I said, "1275 Meigs Place, Apartment 2."

One of the men said, "That's right down the street."

We pulled out of the sally port. It took them 5 minutes to get me in front of my house. The man looked on the paper and dialed my mother's number. She answered on the second ring.

The man said, "Ms. Mayo? We are outside with your son. He's going to bring a paper so you can sign and I want him to bring it back."

She said, "Okay" and they both hung up.

He passed me the paper, I got out of the truck, walked to the front door, walked up the stairs, twisted the knob, and the door was open. My mother was in the living room on the couch. I gave her the paper and she signed it. I walked back down the stairs, went to the truck, and gave the paper back to the man.

I said, "Thanks ya'll."

He said, "You're welcome. But you seem like a good kid. I don't want to see you again in a place like that."

I said, "Okay."

They pulled off. I walked back upstairs to my house, closed, and locked the door. I went into my room and went to sleep.

The next morning I woke up around 11:00 a.m., took a shower, and brushed my teeth. When I was done, I put on my H & M black skinny jeans and my black Polo shirt with the red horse with my black and red Jordans. I went in the kitchen and made myself some Cap'n Crunch cereal. When I was done, I put my bowl in the sink and I told my mother I was leaving out.

She said, "Aight. But, don't get in any more trouble."

I said, "OK, Ma."

I left out the door and walked to Coda's house. When I knocked on Coda's door, his mother asked, "Who is it?"

I said, "It's Lil B Ma."

She opened the door and said, "Coda told me what happened yesterday.

I'm glad you're home. You don't need to be locked up. You need to be out here for your little sister and your mother."

I said, "I know." Then I asked, "Where's Coda at?"

"He's outside somewhere."

"Oh, aight. I'm about to see if I see him."

"Ok."

I walked around by the Northeast Market. He was not right there. Then I walked behind the Northeast Market to Smiley's house. Coda and Smiley were on Smiley's front porch.

I yelled out, "Coda!"

He looked and said, "You home?"

"Yeah Bruhh. I got to go to court next Wednesday."

He said, "True."

I said, "Bruhh, I knew them two ladies were undercovers."

"Me too."

"Bruh, you still got that money?"

"Yeah, but I spent like $10."

"Aight, you good. How much you got left though?"

"Like $50."

"Aight, bet. Do you have a jay or a cigarette?"

"Yeah, I got both."

"Fire that jay up then," I said.

"Aight, I'm about to go to the store and get a roll-up."

We both walked over to the Circle 7, right beside the Northeast Market.

Coda walked in. I stood outside of the door for 5 minutes, waiting on him. When he came out, Derico was walking from behind the Kovack's Liquor Store.

He yelled my name, "Lil B."

I looked and said, "What's up Derico?"

"Nothing, coolin. I got a jay with nobody to smoke with and no roll up."

"You smoke?"

"Yeah, can you get a roll up?"

"Yeah, hold on."

I gave Coda $1.25 and told him to get another roll up. He walked back into the store, got one, and came back out and said, "Where are we smoking at?"

I said, "N***, you must be crazy, you know where we're smoking at- the Dungeon."

"Aight."

Then all three of us walked behind Smiley's house to the Dungeon. That's where I like to smoke at because it's quiet and the police do not come back there. I told Coda to roll the first jay. When he was done rolling, I threw him the lighter and he lit the jay and passed it to me. I hit the jay and passed it to Derico.

When we were done smoking that jay I told Derico to pass me his tree so I can break it down. He gave me the tree, and I started to break the weed down. When I was done, I gave Coda the weed so he could roll the jay. When he was done rolling, he sparked the jay and we all got higher. When we were done smoking, we all walked back on Simms Place. My little cousin Decarlos, aka Loss, was walking down the street.

He said, "Cuzzo, what you about to do?"

I said, "Nothing. What about you?"

"I'm about to go see this girl and you know the rest."

"True . . . you better use a condom."

"I know, N***"

"I was just telling you."

Then we started to play fight. When we were done playing, he left and said he'd see me later on, or tomorrow.

I said, "Aight cuzzo, you be careful."

He said, "Aight" and walked off.

I walked to the store where Coda was at. When I got close to Coda, he said, "Where Loss going?"

"He said he was going over a girl's house."

"True."

It was about 6:00 pm. I told Coda, "I'm going in the house because I got court tomorrow."

"Aight. Good luck."

"Thank you, Bruhh. But I'll see you tomorrow."

"Aight. I hope so."

It took me about 10 minutes to get to my house on Meigs Place. When I walked up, my mother, Piggy, Ooni, and my little sister were on the porch.

I said, "What's up ya'll?"

They said, "What's up Lil' B?"

"Nothin', coolin. About to go in the house and get ready for court tomorrow." Everybody said they wished me luck.

"Thank ya'll." I asked Piggy if she had a cigarette.

She said, "Yeah. Go in my house and open my drawer by the closet and get two cigarettes."

"Aight, are both of them for me?"

"B, didn't you just ask me for a cigarette?"

"Yeah."

"Okay then."

I walked in her house, went in the drawer, got the two cigarettes, walked back outside, and went in my house and laid on my bed. I was thinking about what was going to happen to me in court tomorrow. I hoped they don't try and lock me up because of the little bit of weed I had. I got off my bed because I heard my little sister calling me from outside.

I went to the window, "What, Shay?"

"What you doing?"

"Nothing."

"Can you bring my bike down here for me?"

"Okay, I got you."

"Aight."

I went in the back to my little sister's room and got her pink and purple bike. I took it outside for her.

She said, "Thank you."

"You're welcome Shay." I turned towards my mother. She was sitting on the steps talking to Piggy.

I said, "Excuse me, Ma. Can I see your phone?"

She said, "Yeah" and passed it to me.

I went back upstairs and went in my room. Then I remembered I still had my weed and my coke on me. I put it in my hiding spot in my closet. When I was done with that, I lit my cigarette, went in the living room, and started to watch TV. "Good Times" was on. That is one of my favorite shows to watch. My mother, Piggy, Ooni, and my little sister stayed outside for at least another hour or two.

I heard somebody call me, so I looked out my living room window and it was my mother. She asked me to come get Shay's bike.

I said, "Okay Ma."

I went outside to get my little sister's bike. Then I went in the house and put it back in her room. I walked to my room and dialed Aleah's number. The phone rang a couple of times.

She answered, "Hello."

I said, "Yeah, what's up, boo?"

"Nothing, in the house, about to eat."

"True."

"Why have you not called me in a couple of days?"

"I got locked up for selling weed."

"Why you out there selling weed?"

"Money don't grow on trees. I got to get it the best way I can."

"That don't mean go out and sell drugs."

"You right, but what have you been up to?"

"Nothin', coolin.'"

"That's all you can do these days. I got court tomorrow, so if they lock me up I'm going to call you when I get down YSC."

"I hope they don't lock you up. But I wish you luck."

"Thank you, boo. But I'm about to take a shower, eat, and get my clothes out for tomorrow. I'll call you tomorrow if they don't lock me up."

She said, "Okay" and the phone call ended.

I heard the door close and lock, so I looked out of my room. It was my mother and my little sister. I looked at the phone and it was 10:25 p.m. I went to my closet and got out a white shirt, some socks, and my pajama pants. I walked to the bathroom and turned the shower on. Before I closed the door, my mother yelled, "Give me my phone."

I went back in my room, got the phone, and took it to her. Then, I went back and got in the shower. I was in the shower for about 30 minutes before I got out. When I got out, I dried off, put my underwear, my shirt, my socks, and my pajama pants on. I went in my room, put some deodorant on, brushed my hair, and then went in the kitchen and made a Hot Pocket. When I was done, I peeped in my mother's room and she and my sister were sleeping. I made sure the doors and windows were locked, went in my room, ate, and put the plate in the sink.

■■ ■■

The next morning I woke up at 7:30. My court date was at 10:00. When I got up, I went in the bathroom, washed my face, and brushed my teeth. I went in my mother's room to see if she was up. But she was already up, so I walked back to my room and went to my closet to get some clothes to wear to court. I picked out my blue and white button down H & M shirt with my black Zara jeans and my black and blue Jordans. When I was done picking my clothes out, I started to put them on. After I got dressed, I walked to my mother's room to see if she was dressed. She and my little sister were ready; it was about 8:15.

She asked, "Lil B, are you ready?"

I said, "Yeah, Ma" and we all walked out. We walked to the D8 bus stop on Montello Avenue, just one block away. When we got to the bus stop we waited for five or ten minutes before the bus

came. We got on and rode to Union
Station. When our stop came, we got off
and walked five blocks to the District of
Columbia court building. We stood in line
for a couple of minutes to get inside.

Once we got in, we walked to JM-1, that's
the court room where my case was
supposed to be. My mother, my little
sister, and I sat down in front of the
courtroom to see Judge Ross. Now it was
about 9:25 a.m. My lawyer walked up to
my mother and me and said,
        "They threw the case out, so you
don't need to go in the courtroom."
I was happy.
        My mother said, "Okay."
We all left. We walked to the X2 bus stop.
As soon as we got to the bus stop, the X2
pulled up. We got on the bus. We got off
on 19th and Benning Road, right in front of
the Wings n' More Wings to go to my
grandmother's house. She lived behind

the Wings carry-out. Once we got in front of her house, I rang the doorbell.

My Uncle Mayo answered the door and said, "What's up, ya'll?"

My Uncle Mayo is brown-skinned with facial hair, low haircut. He has a good personality. He likes to smoke weed and drink liquor all day. He is my grandmother's brother.

My mother and I said, "Nothing, coolin."

My mother explained, "We were just at the court building, but they threw his case out."

Mayo said, "That's good."

I walked upstairs to see my grandmother. When I came face to face with her I said,

"What's up, grandma?"

She said, "What's up? What are you doing here?"

"Nothing. My mother, Shay, and I came to see you."

"Where they at?"

"Downstairs with Mayo."

"Aight. I'm about to come down there."

I turned around and went back downstairs where my mother, Shay Shay, and Uncle Mayo were.

∎∎∎

When I got down there, I said, "Ma, Grandma said she'll be down in a little bit."

"Aight."

It took my grandmother about five minutes to come downstairs. When she finally got downstairs, she sat in her chair that's in the kitchen and told my mother to turn the TV on. My mother turned the TV to the stories; all the ladies like to watch those shows for some reason. Then my grandmother asked me if I was hungry.

∎∎∎

I said, "No."

She told me to ask my little sister.

I said, "Okay."

I walked in the living room and asked Shay if she was hungry.

She said, "Yeah."

I went back and told my grandmother that Shay said yes.

"Aight," she said and started to make her a sandwich. When she was done, she told me to take it to her. I walked to the living room and gave it to her.

She said, "Thank you, brother."
I said, "You welcome, Shay" and went back in the kitchen with my mother, my Uncle Mayo, and my grandmother.
As I was walking back in, they all were laughing.

I said, "Ma, can I use your phone?"

She said, "Yeah" and passed it to me.
I walked back in the living room where Shay was at and asked, "Shay, you all right?"

"Yeah."

Then I laid on the couch and dialed Aleah's number.

When she answered I said, "What's up, boo?"

She said, "Nothing. How did court go?"

"We did not even go in the court room. My lawyer came to me and said they threw the case out."

"Oh that's good. I bet you're happy, huh?"

I said, "You know it. Where you at?"

"In the house. What about you?"

"I'm over my grandmother's house."

"Oh, true."

"What you doing today?"

"Nothing, about to eat something."

"You always eating. You're going to get fat."

"No, I'm not."

"Aight, but I'm going to call you later."

She said, "Aight, I love you."
I said, "I love you too."
Then the phone call ended.

My mother called Shay and me and said,
        "Ya'll come on, we're about to
leave."
Shay and I walked to the front door where
my mother, my Uncle Mayo, and my
grandmother were waiting.
My little sister and I gave my grandmother
a hug and a kiss and said, "We'll see you
later, grandma."
        She said, "Okay, I love you all."
        We both yelled out, "We love you
too!"
My mother, my sister, my uncle, and I left
out of the house and walked to the liquor
store on Benning Road. They got some
New Amsterdam. We walked up 19th
Street, made a left on H Place, made a
right into the alley, and made a left into
the gates. We were in our old

neighborhood, down the street from 21ˢᵗ where we used to live. My mother and Uncle Mayo's older friends were outside smoking weed and drinking liquor. As we got closer, my mother's friends came up to her and asked her where she had been.

She said, "I've been in the cut."

I said, "Ma, I'll be back later."

"Aight, I'm going to be leaving around 6:30."

I said, "I'll be back by then. But what time is it?"

"It's 3:00."

I said, "Okay- I love you."

She said, "I love you too."

I walked out of the alley, made a left on H Place, then a right on 19ᵗʰ St. As I was walking down the street, I saw Tray-Tray, both of the twins, Loss, Keyon, V-Man, and Trayvell.

They all called out, "What's up, Lil B?"

I said, "Nothing, just came from court, about 3 or 4 hours ago."

They all said, "True."

Tray-Tray asked, "Do you want to go up Brown with us to the basketball court?" Brown is a school in our neighborhood. School was out for the summer, so we could go up there and play ball whenever we wanted.

I said, "Yeah, come on."

We all walked up H Street to Langston Terrace, made a left down the ramp, and made a right by Charles Young Elementary School. When we came to the T in the street, we made a left and walked halfway down 23rd Street and there was the court, on the right. There were a lot of people on the basketball court that day.

When we got on the court, we saw some of our hood men.

They said, "Lil B, ya'll, come over here, we're about to play a game of 4 on 4."

I said, "Aight" and we all walked over where they were.

Don, who is brown-skinned with dreads said, "Lil B, pick against me."

I said, "All right, I got V-Man."

Don said, "I got Loss."

"I got Keyon and Trayvell."

"I got Justin and we got the ball first."

I said, "Aight."

We started to play. At the end of the game, the score was 14 to 16. We lost, but we took it on the chin.

I said, "Ya'll, I'm about to go back around the way."

They said, "Aight, we'll see you later."

It took me 5 minutes to get back down 19th. I walked to where I left my mother at. She was still out back with her friends.

I walked up to her and said, "Ma, you ready?"

She said, "Yeah, we got a ride."

I said, "Aight. Bet."

One of my mother's friends took my mother, my uncle, my little sister and me back to our house. It took 10 to 15 minutes to get back around Trinidad. When we got in front of my house, we all got out and yelled, "Thank You". We walked up the stairs and went into the house. I went in my room and went to sleep because I was tired.

The next morning I woke up and called Aleah. The phone rang three times and she said hello.

"What's up, Boo?"

She said, "Nothin', coolin'."

"True. Oh, I miss you."

"I miss you too. What you doing?"

"Nothing, just woke up. Where you at?" I asked her.

"I'm in the house on Holbrook."

"True. Can I see you later on?"

"Yeah."

"Aight, I'm going to call you when I get outside."

She said, "Aight."

The phone call ended, and I went in my mother's room to see what she was doing. She was lying on the bed, watching Criminal Minds with my little sister Shay.

I said, "Ma, what you doing?"

She said, "Nothin', coolin, watching TV."

"Yeah, I can see that."

"Why you ask me then if you can see me watching TV?"

"I don't know. What you doing today?"

"Nothing, probably go on the front porch and cool it with Piggy and Ooni."

I said, "True" and I walked back to my room and went in my closet. I picked out my H & M shorts with my pink, green, and blue Polo shirt with my pink & white 990s.

After I put my clothes and stuff on I said, "Ma, I'm gone."

She said, "Aight."

I left out of the house and went to Coda's house. I knocked on his back door, and he yelled, "Who is it?"

"It's Lil B," I answered and he opened the door right away, with a cigarette in his hand.

I said, "Let me hit that."

He passed it to me. I took a hit and asked,

"Bruhh, what's the move today?"

"I don't know."

"What time are you going outside?"

"In a little bit," Coda answered.

I said, "Aight." Then I passed him the cigarette back.

He said, "Lil B, spark this jay of pack" and he threw it to me.

Then I sparked it. I was high off of two hits. I passed Coda the jay and said, "That's some gas."

He said, "I'm hip. My mother's friend gave me that jay earlier."

"Say kill."

"Kill."

I said, "Bruhh, let's go outside."

He said, "Aight, hold up."

Then he walked into his mother's room and said, "Ma, I'm about to go outside."

She said, "Aight."

He walked back to where I was and said, "C'mon."

We both walked out the back door. As we were walking down the alley, we started laughing at this female running down the alley- completely naked. We kept on walking over there by the Circle 7 and the Northeast Market. When we got over there, a lot of people were outside. It was around 1:30 or 2 in the afternoon. I walked behind the Circle 7 onto Simms Place. The whole Simms Place had people outside. Some people were playing horseshoes, while some were just talking to each other. In my head, I was thinking, "Damn, some of these females look good who are walking past."

I walked back to Coda and said, "Bruhh, I'm about to walk back to my house, I'll be right back- in like 20 minutes."

He said, "Aight. I'm going to be out here for a minute."

"Aight, bet."

When I got to my house, my front porch was **live**. It was crowded with people. I said "What's up?" to everybody first.

Then, I asked my mother if I could see her phone.

She said, "Yeah" and she passed it to me.

I dialed Aleah's number. She answered.

I said, "Boo, where you at?"

She said, "At the Rec."

"Aight. I'll be up there in a little bit."

"Okay, see you then."

We hung up and I called out to my mother, "Ma, I'll be back later."

She said, "Aight, then bring me my phone."

I walked to the front of the Rec. Nobody was outside, so I walked inside and the first person I saw was Aleah. She walked up to me, gave me a hug, and said,

"What's up, Bae?"

I said, "Nothing. Coolin."

"True."

I asked her, "What you eat today?"

She said, "Some chicken and pizza."

"That sounds good."

"Yeah, What'd you eat today?"

"A sandwich."

"Oh. What'd you do today?"

"Nothing for real. I went to see what Coda was doing and that's it."

"True. You always with Coda, he must be your right hand man or something."

"Yeah, you know it. Where your sister at?"

"In here somewhere."

Then Derico came up to us and said, "Lil B, what's up?"

I said, "Nothing, coolin. How long you been outside?"

"Not that long."

"True. What you about to do?"

"I don't know. What about you?"

"I'm going to chill with my girl for a little bit, then go back in the house."

He asked, "Oh, who your girl?"

I said, "Aleah."

"Oh. That's why you two are always together."

I started to laugh.

Then he said, "I'm going to talk to ya'll later."

Aleah and I both said, "Aight."

I said, "Boo- when are you going to come over my house and meet my mother?"

Aleah answered, "I don't know."

I said, "True" and she asked me the same thing.

"When you want me to?" I asked.

"I'm going to see."

"Aight. But how long are you going to be out here at the Rec?"

"Like 10 to 20 minutes."

I said, "Aight but I'm about to go in the house and chill with my mother and little sister."

She said good-bye and gave me a kiss and a hug.

I said, "I love you, boo."

She said, "I love you too" and went back into the Rec center. When I got back to my house, it was 5:00 in the afternoon. My mother, little sister, Piggy and Ooni were still on the porch.

When I walked up, I said, "Ma, what'd you cook because I'm hungry?"

She said, "Some french fries and fried chicken."

"Oh yeah. I'm about to go and crush."

"Make sure you wash your hands."

"Aight Ma, I'm not stupid." Then I went in the house. I washed my hands in the bathroom and went to the kitchen to make a plate for myself. Then I walked in my room, sat on the bed, turned the TV on to Criminal Minds, and started to eat. When I was done eating, I put the plate in the sink, walked back in my room, took my clothes off and lay on the bed.

The next morning I woke up and went to the bathroom to brush my teeth and wash my face. When I was done, I walked in my mother's room and she was not in there. In my head, I'm thinking, "Where is my mother?"

I turned around and walked back in my room and put on some shorts, a shirt, and my shoes. When I was done, I heard a lot of people talking out back. I walked to the back door to see who it was. It was my mother, Ooni, Piggy, and the whole complex. Everyone was outside. My sister Shay walked up to me and asked me how long I'd been awake.

I said, "For like 10 or 15 minutes."

She said, "Oh."

I said, "How long have you all been out back?"

She said, "For an hour and a half."

"True."

Then I walked to my mother and said, "Ma, I'm about to go down the street."

She said, "Aight."

I left.

I walked to Coda's house and knocked on his door. Somebody said, "Who is it?"

"It's Lil' B."

The door opened and it was his mother.

I asked, "Ma, where Coda at?"

As she was walking away from the door, she said, "In his room, cleaning up."

I walked in, closed the door, and locked it. Then, I walked down the hallway to Coda's room. He was mopping his floor.

I said, "What's up, bruhh?"

He said, "Nothin' coolin', trying to clean my room. But how long have you been in here?"

"I just walked in the door."

"Oh, but what happened to you the other day? You ain't never come back."

"My bad. I got caught up doing something for my mother."

"Oh, true."

"What time you going outside?"

"In like 5 minutes. Let me get the rest of my room straight."

I said, "Aight" and walked to the living room, sat on the couch. The BET Awards were on. I was looking at TV for about ten minutes.

Coda came in and said, "C'mon lil' bruhh'."

I got up and we walked out the back door. Coda and I walked down the alley until we got on Mount Olivet Road. We made a left and walked over by the Circle 7. When we got over there, Smiley and Darren were sitting on the wall.

They both asked, "What's up?" to me and Coda.

Coda and I said, "Nothin' just coolin."

EPILOGUE

In the next five years, I want to have a big house, with a wife and kids. I want my mother and little sister to come and live with me. I want to move out of D.C. to Paris, France because in D.C. you have to look over your shoulder too much, worrying about who is going to rob you. I would like to move to Paris because you don't have to look over your shoulder as much. It seems like a peaceful place to live.

In the next five years, I want to be a Navy Seal. I want to be a Navy Seal because I like what they do. I like the way they jump out of planes and stay under water for a long time. Also, I like how they killed Osama bin Laden. But, if that doesn't work out, then I would like to be an EMT or a firefighter. I want to be an EMT or a firefighter because I want to help people who need medical attention.